BREAKING THE BARRIERS

Keys to Unlocking Inner Peace

Rev. John Clark Mayden, Jr.

Breaking the Barriers
Copyright © 2015 by **Rev. John Clark Mayden, Jr.**. All rights reserved.

No part of this publication may be reproduced, stored in a retrieval system or transmitted in any way by any means, electronic, mechanical, photocopy, recording or otherwise, without the prior permission of the author except as provided by USA copyright law.

All characters appearing in this work are fictitious. Any resemblance to real persons, living or dead, is purely coincidental.

The opinions expressed by the author are not necessarily those of Revival Waves of Glory Books & Publishing.

Published by Revival Waves of Glory Books & Publishing
PO Box 596| Litchfield, Illinois 62056 USA
www.revivalwavesofgloryministries.com

Revival Waves of Glory Books & Publishing is committed to excellence in the publishing industry.

Book design copyright © 2015 by Revival Waves of Glory Books & Publishing. All rights reserved.

Paperback: 978-1-60796-601-2
Hardcover: 978-1-329-14625-9

Published in the United States of America

Table of Contents

Introduction 5
Purpose of the Book 7
The Three D's 8
Target Audience 9
Prologue 10
Overcoming Despair 12
    The Chains Are Broken 13
    Be Still and Wait 16
    Imagine 19
    Ignoring the Noise 22
    A Made Up Mind 25
    The Path to Peace 27
    Hope for the Silent Sufferer 30
Dealing with Disappointment 34
    From Victim to Victor 35
    I Am Letting Go!!! 38
    Secure In the Lord 41
    Moving Beyond Disappointment 44
    I Am Moving On 47
    Tackling Disappointment 50
    The Power of Praise 53

MANAGING DEPRESSION 56
    "Peace in the Storm" 57
    Overcoming Grief 60
    Help Needed 63
    God, Help Them 66
    Depression Isn't Here to Stay 69
    Don't Give Up Poem 72
    I Am Holding On (Poem) 75
About The Author 77
Acknowledgement 78

Introduction

Despite the whirlwind of confusion, stress and drama you may face in life, inner peace is still possible. Inner peace is possible because it is "not the absence of conflict from life, but the ability to cope with it" by trusting and leaning on the Lord Jesus Christ. So, it should come as no surprise that we find these timely words spoken from Our Lord Jesus Christ: [27] Peace I leave with you my peace I give you. I do not give to you as the world gives. Do not let your hearts be troubled and do not be afraid." This Biblical account records the words spoken by Jesus to his disciples preparing them for his death. He encourages his fearful and stressed out disciples as they are facing the threat of persecution by the Romans to receive the peace that he is leaving for them. In addition, the Scripture speaks volumes to us because it reveals that it is the will of God that we experience true peace of mind. As well, this text suggests that peace is attainable by letting go and moving forward from the unhealthy thoughts and negative emotions so that we are in a position to enjoy life. In essence, the Scripture provides us the blueprint for breaking through the barriers in our lives and aid us in fulfilling our destiny.

Purpose of the Book

This topical devotional resource is the first of a three volume series that aims to provide the reader with spiritual keys to help them overcome common barriers that prevent them from experiencing inner peace. These keys are intended to help the reader unlock the door of inner peace and move forward in life and get unstuck from the ruts of sadness, frustration and inner turmoil. As a result of experiencing peace, the reader is released to become the person that God wants them to be and achieve the purpose that God has for their life.

Ultimately, the central message of the book is that true inner peace comes with knowing Christ is present with us through our adversities. Moreover, in the midst of our troubles, trials and turmoil we can still have an inner peace because we are not facing these challenges alone. Thus, inner peace is the realization that the power of Christ will sustain us in our hard times. So, hopefully, you will find the twenty one keys and inspirations helpful and experience transformation, healing and a breakthrough in your life.

The Three D's

Barriers are distractions or roadblocks that **prevent us** from being the person that God wants and achieving the purpose that God has for our lives. There are many barriers that hinder people from experiencing inner peace. In this book, I will focus on The Three D's of Despair, Disappointment, and Depression as everyday barriers that can disconnect us from God.

I write from personal experience with The Three D's, as they still have the power to leave me emotionally drained and stressed, robbing me of precious moments in my life. Finding inner peace is a daily process for me and I must renew my mind each day to receive the peace, joy and fulfillment that God wants for me.

One night, while watching television, I heard the voice of the Lord tell me to write down "Breaking the Barriers" as the title for this book. God wants me to share with you these keys that help me in my struggle with The Three D's. Hopefully, this book will help you break these three barriers and move from a place of pain to God's promise.

Target Audience

This resource is intended for individuals, small groups and Bible Study groups that are seeking spiritual, emotional and physical restoration and healing.

Layout

The layout of the book is as follows: there are three chapters with seven inspirational messages addressing each barrier. At the top of each page, there is a title for the inspirational message, after each title is an image related to the message. Below the image is a spiritual key in the form of a key sign with the spiritual principle next to it. After the message, there is a Scripture at the bottom of each page. At the beginning of the next page, there is an action step intended to put the principle (key) into practice. After each action step there is a question maybe two for the reader to ponder which aims to help apply the inspirational message.

Prologue

Absolutely, without a shadow of a doubt you can break through The Three D's of Despair, Disappointment and Depression. The Bible has many remedies for The Three D's that will be discussed within this book which include: the position of both our mind and our body, seeking comfort in the Scriptures, and offering encouragement to others.

Overcoming Despair

The Chains Are Broken

Key: Surrender your burden to God.

The best way to deal with despair is to surrender your burden to the Lord. Surrender involves giving up. Just the other day, I listened to a Christian Recovery Broadcast on the radio. The host of the show made an excellent point about surrender being the first step toward recovering from any addiction. He went onto to state that a drug addict or alcoholic must first acknowledge that they cannot overcome their addiction alone. In other words, the addict must give their situation over to God to begin the healing process.

Surrender helps remove the chains of despair and hopelessness. In addition, surrender allows trust and encouragement to escort you in your situations. Therefore, you can leave your problems at God's feet, knowing that God will work the situation out in your favor. You now can experience peace and have healthy relationships now all because you surrender your burdens to the Lord.

Cast Your Burden on the Lord, and He will sustain you. Psalm 55:22 (English Standard Version).

Application

Action Step: Make a list of things that stress you out. For example, you may be stressing about a member of your family that has frequent run-ins with the law. Commit to daily praying for that family member or whatever it is that bothers you.

1.

2.

3.

1. What are some things that you can surrender in your life to grow closer to God?

Be Still and Wait

 Key: Listen for God's response.

In our prayer life, we may speak to God, but don't listen. We tell God, what is on our mind, but don't always have the patience to listen to God's response to our situation. Therefore, we have our minds made up about how we are going to handle a situation and the prayer really begins to be more of habit rather than truly seeking God. And the question is: what is the point of praying if we are too impatient or unwilling to await God's response?

Not listening to God's response would be like a pilot contacting the control tower prior to take off, but not waiting to hear the message: "You are cleared for take-off" and just, impulsively, taking off on his own. That pilot would place his life as well as the passengers of the plane in jeopardy.

In a spiritual sense, when we don't listen for God's response in our lives, we set ourselves up for hurt, pain and pitfalls. From personal experience, I know that it is so much easier to take that extra time and wait to hear from God than to try to do things on your own strength. I am imploring you to listen to God's response to your prayer before moving on with a decision.

Be still before the LORD and wait patiently for him do not fret when people succeed in their ways, when they carry out their wicked schemes. Psalm 37:7 New International Version.

Application

Action: After you pray, spend time still and waiting in silence for God to respond.

1.

2.

3.

1. What are some areas in your life that you are still waiting to hear from God?

Imagine

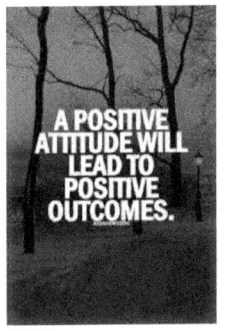

 Key: Envision a Positive Outcome

God has given you the authority over the outcomes of your circumstances. Envisioning a positive outcome is the key to situations improving in your life. Let me share with you a story that paints an accurate and compelling picture of envisioning a positive outcome.

There is a story about a man who was incarcerated and wrongly convicted for murder. After serving a five year sentence, he had a review hearing before the judge. Prior to the hearing, his attorney noticed his calm demeanor. When asked about his demeanor the prisoner responded that he is calm because he envisioned his release from jail because he was not guilty. He pictured that he would walk out of the courtroom a free man without chains confining his hands. Accordingly, he was released from prison.

Interestingly enough, mentally and emotionally he was already set free from confinement because of his mindset and his foresight. So, today envision a positive outcome. Believe that things will get better.

"Everything is possible for one who believes." Mark 9:23 NIV

Application

Action Step: Write down three hardships. Right beside these hardships, write down three positive outcomes that you envision taking place in your life.

1.

2.

3.

1. What is a positive outcome that you are looking forward to happening?

Ignoring the Noise

 Key: Ignore Negativity

Do you have dreams, but are afraid to pursue them because you have been discouraged by what others had to say? Have their negativity weighed you down? If the answer is yes, this message will encourage your spirit.

The best way to deal with negativity is to ignore it. Ignoring it means not allowing the negative comments and words around you to penetrate your heart. Don't allow it to stop you from moving forward with the goals and plans that God has for your life.

Just the other day, I heard a story about a former NFL great. The NFL player had to overcome his critics that pointed to his lack of size and speed as barriers to him being a successful NFL player. Not only did he prove his critics wrong, but he ended up becoming one of the greatest Wide Receivers in NFL history. But the greater story is that this football player used his fame and football experience as a platform to share the Gospel with other players. The secret to his success was that he ignored the negativity.

In closing, we must stop allowing the negativity of people to **determine our destiny.** Too often, we are bruised by the hurtful words others say and stop pursuing the plans that God has for our lives. So, when people say negative things about you, don't believe them.

Do everything without grumbling or arguing, [15] so that you may become blameless and pure, "children of God without fault in a warped and crooked generation."[c] Then you will shine among them like stars in the sky. (Phil. 2:14-15 NIV).

Application

Action Step: Write down your goals and dreams. Write beside each goal what the voice of negativity in your mind says about you achieving that goal. Next, cross out what the voice of negativity, says and you will just have your goal on the page.

1.

2.

3.

1. What goals or dreams have you allowed someone to discourage you from reaching?

A Made Up Mind

STRENGTH IS A MATTER OF THE MADE-UP MIND.

 Key: Choose Peace

If I was a betting man, I would wager that I have lost countless hours over my lifetime to despair. But, one thing I have learned is that the more I stressed and worried my circumstance did not get any better. However, I have learned that inner Peace is a choice. We can either choose peace or choose to worry and fret over life. The decision is ours.

Choosing peace is really deciding to set our minds on things that are positive and Godly. For an example, thinking about the good times that I share with the individual helps puts my mind at ease when inevitable differences arise in personal relationships.

You will keep in perfect peace those whose minds are steadfast, because they trust in you. Isaiah 26:3. New Living Translation.

Application

Action Step: Take a break from everything that stresses you out. For example, if work is stressful take time off.

1. What are situations and things that trouble you?

2. How might choosing peace look in your situation?

The Path to Peace

 Key: Silence equals peace.

Peace is attainable in silence. Not through the hustling and bustling of life, nor constantly running around taking care of tasks after tasks, but in silence will peace come into our lives. The text below makes the connection between silence and peace. In essence, the Scripture encourages us to not complain when things do not go our way, but to be silent. When we are silent, we are able to hear and receive a Word from the Lord and become empowered.

Psalm 62, presents us with King David being empowered by the Presence of God as a result of silently listening and waiting on God during his prayer time. During the time of the text, there were mean people that planned to kill King David so he prayed and waited for the Lord in silence. Subsequently, the verse ends with David receiving the peace of the Lord. If we want to receive peace from the Lord, let's wait to hear from God in silence.

The fruit of that righteousness will be peace its effect will be quietness and confidence forever. Isaiah 32:17 New Living Translation.

Application

Action Step: Take a couple of minutes out of each day and sit in silence waiting to hear a Word from the Lord. Write down what you hear God saying to you.

1.

2.

3.

1. Are you able to hear the voice of the Lord today?

Hope for the Silent Sufferer

Key: Acknowledge your struggle to the Lord.

Hold On and don't give up. Let these words resonate within your spirit. You are more valuable than what you are going through. I know you can't see it, but change is around the corner. How do I know? I know because I have been there. I have been in a place where I have been so depressed that I didn't want to get out of bed. Life just seemed to strain me, but, acknowledging my struggle before the Lord helped me overcome my suffering. Day, I had to tell God, what bothers and taxes me. Specifically, I told the Lord that I am tired of being down and not having the joy and the Lord continued to lift my burden from me. Even today, when I get sad and feel down I just tell God, what is bothering me and God constantly uplifts my spirit. In conclusion, I want to tell you to hang in there and don't quit. Acknowledge your struggle before the Lord and watch God work that situation out in your favor.

I call on the LORD in my distress, and he answers me. Psalm 120:1 NIV

Application

Action Step: If you are feeling suicidal or homicidal get help. Please call The National Suicide Prevention Lifeline at 1-800-273-8255. Seek the counsel of a Pastor or a Professional Counselor.

1. How can acknowledging your struggle help you with despair?

Dealing with Disappointment

From Victim to Victor

🔑 Key: Stretch Your Hand to the Lord

Many of us have been guilty of allowing our circumstances to dictate our attitudes. As a result of experiencing abuse, neglect and any form of trauma, we may adopt the mindset that we are victims. We may begin to walk with our heads hanging down. We hold onto the belief that woe is us. But, the Scripture below navigates us through the process of going from a victim to a victor.

We become victors when we stretch out our hands to the Lord. Stretching our hands to the Lord, positions us to receive power from on High to help us through life. Therefore, we are empowered and equipped to handle our problems because God is actively supporting and backing us.

The result of stretching our hands to the Lord is releasing. We are releasing our problems to God's capable hands. For example, when a prisoner is released from prison the first thing that happens is their handcuffs are opened. Well, in a spiritual sense when we stretch our hands to the Lord our spiritual handcuffs are opened and we are free from oppression. So, the next time we are going through hardships we must stretch our hands to the Lord and watch God restore us.

"And he looked around at them with anger, grieved at their hardness of heart, and said to the man, "Stretch out your hand." He stretched it out, and his hand was restored. "Mark 3:5 (ESV)

Application

<u>Action Step: Continue to seek God in prayer, meditation, praise and worship and giving.</u>

1. What keeps you from stretching your hands out and giving your burdens to the Lord?

<u>I Am Letting Go!!!</u>

🔑 Key: Letting go past hurt and pain will help you move forward in life.

"Forget what lies behind." You might be sitting there thinking you don't know what I have done. I have done some things that are unforgivable. I have already dug my grave and now I have to go lie in it. Let's take a quick look back at the author of this letter of Philippians past.

Paul, the author of the text was an accomplice to murder to many of the early Christians. He was responsible for many murders and most notably the execution of the first Christian martyr Stephen. His goal was to torture and rid the earth of Christianity. Fast forward, he later became the greatest apostle (Church founders) that ever walked the earth and was a prominent figure in the development of the early Christian movement. The key to his remarkable

Christian progression is that he had to let go of the past.

Letting go of the past means we have to stop hitting the rewind button in our lives by revisiting our mistakes. We have to stop letting guilt from past mistakes weight us down because God wants us to let it go. Below is an example of letting it go.

The act of letting go is similar to releasing a balloon into the sky. Once our hands stop holding onto the balloon the balloon begins to ascend upward. Most of the times, people let the balloons go as the balloon deflates because the balloon does not have use any longer. The same balloon analogy may be applied to our lives. We should not hold onto feelings of disappointment because they will keep us in a rut. Instead, we must constantly seek to let go of those things that stress us out. Just let it go.

[13] Brothers and sisters, I know that I still have a long way to go. But there is one thing I do: I forget what is in the past and try as hard as I can to reach the goal before me. Philippians 3:13

Application

Action Step: Buy a balloon and blow it up. Next, visualize that your burdens are a balloon and let the balloon go.

1. What are some things that you are willing to let go?

Secure In the Lord

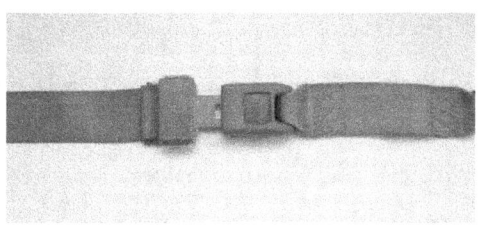

🔑 Key: Security comes by keeping our eyes on the Lord.

Past disappointments may give rise to insecurity in life which affects your ability to have sustained relationships. In other words, you may have experienced broken promises or hurtful things spoken against you. In essence, you may be looking to people in your life for validation and affirmation in an attempt to counter disappointments and hurts of the past. However, the Scriptures encourage us to be secure in the Lord.

Security in the Lord helps us keep our eyes on the Lord, which will help us in our relationships. Think about it when we are able to trust in God, we are in a better position to listen to others and preserve healthy relationships. I can say that depending on God has helped me to nurture my relationships with others because I didn't look at everyone as the enemy. For instance, imagine taking your eyes off the seat belt while trying to secure a baby in a car seat the seat would probably not be secure and the child could get seriously hurt because they were not strapped in the car seat properly.

Spiritually, when we take our eyes off the Lord, we become unstable and experience unnecessary pain. We may become people pleasers and are overly consumed with what others think and say about us. So, the best thing to do is to keep your eyes on The Lord and you will experience security and peace.

I have set the Lord always before me because he is at my right hand, I shall not be shaken. Psalm 16:8

Application

Action Step: When you begin to feel insecure constantly recite this Scripture: "Because you are precious in my eyes, and honored, and I love you,...."[1]

1. How do I remain secure in the Lord?

---

[1] Isaiah 43:4 English Standard Version.

Moving Beyond Disappointment

🔑 Key: Set realistic expectations.

Many times we become disappointed because we set unrealistic expectations. A way that we set these unrealistic expectations is when we compare people. For example, there are marriages that don't work because spouses may compare their spouse with their ex. This comparison is unwarranted and leaves the spouse being compared with a feeling of inadequacy and insufficiency. However, one thing that I have found extremely helpful is to avoid disappointment by setting realistic expectations.

A personal example of setting unrealistic expectations came when I searched for employment a couple of years ago. During that time, I expected a call from my prospective employer the day or day after I applied for the job. Every day, I would be disappointed when I did not hear anything from the employer. But, what helped me through my disappointment was to stop anticipating that I would hear a call from a potential employer within 24 hours of completing the application. Setting realistic expectation greatly assisted me and helped me to stop worrying about things that I could not change.

"I am the vine, you are the branches. If you remain in me and I in you, you will bear much fruit apart from me you can do nothing. John 15:5 New International Version.

Application

Action Step: Write some unrealistic expectations that you have. Besides, the unrealistic expectations write some realistic expectations. For example, an example of an unrealistic expectation may be that you just started working a job and expect to receive a promotion within six months of your hire date. A realistic expectation may be within five years of accepting the position, you expect to be promoted because you have prayed and worked hard. Start to cross the unrealistic expectations off, and work toward the realistic expectations.

1. What unrealistic expectations do I have in my life?

I Am Moving On

🔑 Key: Focus on the solution.

Not too long, I read a story about a distraught, young, married mother, Lucy Blackwell, who was caring for her sick son, Noah Blackwell. Daily, she went to the hospital to visit and spent time with her son. The doctor told Lucy that the only way that her son's life would be saved is if a matching blood type was found. Of course, the mother and the father's blood type did not match the child's. However, the husband located Lucy's estranged father. And as it turned out the grandfather's blood type was a match. The surgery took place and Noah's life was saved.

Now, imagine if Lucy's let her disappointment and displeasure of her father's absence from her life stand in the way of her son getting the treatment that he needed. Noah probably would have died.

On the other hand, Lucy focused on the solution. She focused on her son's health and well-being. In fact, not only was her son's life saved, but she was able to develop a close knit relationship with her father because she was solution centered.

Finally, my brothers and sisters, let's strive to be solution centered people. Let's not focus only on the problem, but look to the strategies that will bring the solution to fruition. Focusing on the solution will help you move past your disappointments in life and allow you to truly thrive and soar and overcome the hardships in life.

And we know that in all things God works for the good of those who love him, who [a] have been called according to his purpose. Romans 8:28 New International Version.

Application

First, reflect on solutions to your issues. Write them down.

1.

2.

3.

1. What does the above story teach you about being solution centered?

Tackling Disappointment

🔑 *Key: Speak a word of affirmation over your situations.*

Speaking a word of affirmation over your situations will drastically change outcomes. Within the past two years, I went to the doctor's office for a routine checkup and my blood pressure was elevated. The medical professionals had concerns and cautioned me to monitor my blood pressure because high blood pressure is hereditary within my family. Shortly after the visit, I recall being very discouraged about my elevated blood pressure, but then I vocally affirmed "with God's help, I will lower my blood pressure." The next time that I went to the doctor's office my blood pressure was normal and I attribute the lower blood pressure to speaking a word of affirmation over my situation.

Speaking the word of affirmation helped me to stop stressing and tensing up my muscles during the blood pressure screening, which would always elevate my pressure in the past. In addition, speaking the word of affirmation helped me to see beyond the high blood pressure to the possibility that God could reduce my blood pressure, but I needed to believe the positive words that I spoke. Therefore, whenever I take a blood pressure exam, I reflect on those strong words of affirmation to alleviate any stress and discomfort.

Lastly, the Scripture encourages us to speak positive and affirmative words because words have power. Words may build up or tear down. In essence, words transform an atmosphere. So, I want to strongly encourage you to speak a word of affirmation over your situation. For example, if you are in a lot of debt say "I will get out of debt with God's help." These words will help you as you begin to modify or change certain habits that have put you in so much debt. Speak affirming words and watch your circumstances improve.

Let no corrupting talk come out of your mouths, but only such as is good for building up, as fits the occasion, that it may give grace to those who hear. Ephesians 4:29 English Standard Version

Application

Action Step: Boldly proclaim positive words today.

1. How will speaking affirmative words help me overcome my battle with discouragement?

The Power of Praise

🔑 Key: Praise God despite how you feel.

Perhaps, you have been told that you will never amount to anything in life. Or you were always picked last to join a team. These two instances can cause one to think low about themselves.

Many teenagers and adults suffer from depression. They stop believing that they matter. But the above Scripture provides hope and encouragement to all dealing with esteem issues. For adults, they may give up on joy. These reactions to sadness really discourage and dishearten people from experiencing pleasure and delight.

A proven Biblical solution is to begin praising God for creating you. Every day, recite "I praise you, for I am fearfully and wonderfully made. Wonderful are your works my soul knows it very well.[2]" This Scripture will help you to begin to value yourself as you begin to see your significance to God.

"I praise you, for I am fearfully and wonderfully made. Wonderful are your works my soul knows it very well." Psalm 139:14 ESV

---

[2] Psalm 139:14 English Standard Version.

Application

Action Step: Sing songs to the Lord before you start your day. Thank God for all His blessings in your life.

1. What are some things that you want to thank God for today?

MANAGING DEPRESSION

"Peace in the Storm"

🗝 Key: Stand on God's promises.

Peace is possible. Let's allow these three words ("Quiet! Be Still[3]") to marinate through our hearts and minds. So, when the winds of worry, stress and anxiety are swirling around in your life, remember that Jesus can calm our storms just like he did in the text. All we have to do is stand on God's promises.

Standing on God's promises will make peace a reality in your life. The action of standing means that you rely and depend on the Word of God. This simply means that even when the situations and circumstances of life become challenging you will not give up because you know what God says. Here is a way that we can better understand the concept of Standing on God's promises. Standing on God's promises is like overcoming many obstacles to get to your destination (IE. Flight delays, road closures,

---

[3] Mark 4:39 ESV

etc.). The point is that no matter what happens in life we should be unmovable and always abiding in Christ because God promises to never leave, fail nor forsake you so that means that when all kinds of chaos and confusion is happening all around you there is still peace.

Peace comes from knowing that the Lord is present in your situation. Peace comes from knowing that your issue is not greater than the strength of God. Peace comes from knowing that "greater is He that is in You than He that is in the world.[4]" Finally, peace comes from knowing that God is in control and that God's "plans are to prosper you and not to harm you and to give you a future with hope.[5]" My brothers and sisters stand on God's promises today.

[39] Jesus stood up and gave a command to the wind and the water. He said, "Quiet! Be still!" Then the wind stopped, and the lake became calm. Mark 4:39 (ESV)

---

[4] I John 4:4 KJV
[5] Jeremiah 29:11

Application

Action: "Meditate on the Word of God, both day and night.[6]"

1. What should you do when you get overwhelmed with discouragement?

---

[6] Psalm 1:2 New International Version.

<u>Overcoming Grief</u>

🔑 Key: Draw comfort and strength from the Lord.

One reason that people are depressed is because they are overtaken by grief which is closely connected with loss. The losses of a loved one, friend or a pet are just a few types of losses that happen during life and greatly upset us. It is hard to come to grips with the fact that someone we are close to being gone.

In my life, I have encountered some key losses such as my maternal grandmother which deeply saddened me. This loss disturbed me because I had a rich relationship with my grandmother. She really taught me how to be a responsible and Godly man. Though she died eight years ago, I still miss her.

Yet, drawing comfort and strength from knowing the Lord is what helps me through my grief because I am able to enjoy the fond memories and lessons that my grandmother taught me. I find reassurance and ease in the fact that the Lord is present with me in my time of sorrow. Therefore, the Lord constantly strengthens and uplifts me when I deal with sadness. Beloved, I encourage you to draw comfort and strength from the Lord.

Blessed are those who mourn, for they will be comforted. Matthew 5:4 New International Version.

Application

Action Steps: Writing a Good Bye Letter may be helpful for those who have lost someone. The purpose of this good - bye letter would be to bring closure about the loss person. After all, the word good-bye is a contraction of the Old English "God be with you".

1. How might you draw strength and comfort from the Lord?

Help Needed

🗝 Key: Connect with a spiritual support system.

There are times when the circumstances of life will overwhelm you. Financial issues, health struggles and problems in the family may be very burdensome. As a result of these burdens, you may feel depressed and at the tipping point of giving up because you feel alone. On the other hand, one of the best ways to handle depression is to connect with a spiritual support system. A small group or Bible Study will provide a safe, healing environment. These settings will provide you with a Christian environment where you can heal, grow and thrive.

In college, I recall a good friend of mine dealt with depression. She felt that friends had turned their back on her, but what helped her was joining Intervarsity Christian Ministry. During her time with Intervarsity, she could share her experiences with other Christians and relax and get away from the things that depressed her. Her spiritual support system helped lift her up at her time of need. So, if you don't have a spiritual support system, please identify and connect with not giving up meeting together, as some are in the habit of doing, but encouraging one another—and all the more as you see the Day approaching. Hebrews 10:25 New International Version.

Application

Action: Ask God to help you identify a few members from your place of worship. As a group, decide to devote sessions to discuss stressful things in your lives.

If you are not part of a church begin to write down names of churches and ask God for guidance as to which church to join.

1. What are some ministries within your church that you feel safe to talk about your depression?

God, Help Them

 KEY: Pray for Others.

At times, we are all overcome with challenges and adversity. We really can get stuck in our rut when we just focus on our problems. We develop a woe is me attitude. The story of Job shows us that Job lost his family, social status and his property. These losses had a cumulative impact and depressed Job. Just how was Job going to recover from his great losses? Well, the answer is surprising.

The book of Job ends with Job praying for his friends. Yes, the same people that discouraged Job from trusting in the Lord. By praying for them, Job took the attention off his personal misery and considered his friends. After Job turned his attention away from self God restored his fortune.

Now, the lesson that we can take home is that God wants us to pray for others in our adversity. I remember times when I felt sad and I stopped wallowing around in my own pity party and directed my attention to others in prayer. As a result, I felt better and encouraged. Praying for others restores lifts up our spirits and that of others. Please pray for someone else today.

After Job had prayed for his friends, the LORD restored his fortunes and gave him twice as much as he had before. Job 42:10 New International Version.

Application

Action: Make a list of friends and love and pray for them people daily.

1.

2.

3.

1. Who can you add to your prayer list today?

Depression Isn't Here to Stay

 KEY: Maintain a positive outlook.

The Apostle Paul was one of the most influential leaders in the Christian Church Movement. He founded many churches and he served God with his whole heart. Despite all of his success in ministry, he still suffered and went through great adversity. His hardships included being shipwrecked, persecuted and imprisoned. Notwithstanding all of his trials, he continued to be a great missionary of the Gospel of Christ. You may be wondering what fueled Paul to continue to spread the Gospel in the face of his difficulties? Paul maintained a positive outlook in spite of his numerous challenges. He realized that his suffering had a purpose. The purpose of his suffering was to eventually see the face of Christ in Heaven.

The key to maintaining a positive outlook is contentment. The word contentment means "ease of mind or satisfied." So, the life application is that we have to come to the place where we are content with our suffering knowing that our suffering is for a purpose. We have to remember that we are afflicted to make us stronger. When we realize that distress serves a purpose, we won't get so stressed out and emotionally exhausted because we know that our hard times are a stepping stone to draw closer to Christ. Let's today strive to maintain a positive outlook on life. [7]

I consider that our present sufferings are not worth comparing with the glory that will be revealed in us. Romans 8:18 New International Version.

---

[7] www.dictionary.reference.com

Application

Action Step: Write down things that the Lord has done in your life.

1.

2.

3.

1. What things keep me from keeping a positive outlook?

Don't Give Up Poem

🔑 Key: Rest in the Presence of the Lord.

Why give up?

Why throw in the towel?

Isn't that what the enemy wants me to do anyway?

Doesn't the devil want me to be so afraid of failure that I don't even try to reach for my dreams?

Aren't I really scared of success?

Then I hear the angel of the Lord telling me to remain in the fight and not quit.

Then Satan whispers in my ear to throw in the towel because people keep dying, those close to me keep lying. So, Satan tries to convince me that there really isn't a point to keep trying.

Then the angel of the Lord revisits me and tells me just like I set the Israelites free from Egyptian captivity, raised Lazarus from the dead and healed the sick I will help you through your mess.

Then Satan whispers: The Lord did it for others, but won't do it for me.

Finally, the Angel of the Lord rebukes Satan and says "Get Behind Thee Satan.[8]"

At last, the Lord, then leaves me with these words: "but those who hope in the LORD will renew their strength. They will soar on wings like eagles, they will run and not grow weary, they will walk and not be faint." Now, I will rest in the Presence of The Lord.

Trust in the Lord with all of your heart and lean not on your own understanding. Proverbs 3:5 NIV

---

[8] Matthew 16:23 New International Version.

Application

Action Step: Identify a quiet place in your residence and daily begin to cry out to God in prayer, praise and confession of sins.

1. Are the some areas in your lives that constantly eat at your spirit?

2. What are you going to do today to help you rest in the presence of God?

I Am Holding On (Poem)

 Key: Accept that God is in control.

No matter what we are going through always remember that God is in control.

The rising of the sun, the blowing of the wind and the roaring waves are constant reminders that God is in control.

Accepting that God is in control means resisting the urge to know all the answers to your situations.

Accepting that God is in control means knowing that all things will be alright.

Accepting that God is in control means realizing the hand of God at work in our lives.

I form light and create darkness, I make well-being and create calamity, I am the Lord, who does all these things. Isaiah 45:7 English Standard Version.

Application

Action Step: Determine whether you spend too much time trying to figure things out or allow God to work things out.

1. What does God being in control mean to you?

About The Author

Rev. John Clark Mayden, Jr. is a Christian and Pastor of the Mount Zion United Methodist Church located in Upperco, MD. He is married to Minister Kirstyn Mayden.

If you have not accepted Jesus make the decision today. It will be the best decision of your life. Pray this prayer:

Dear Jesus,

I confess my sins to you.

I invite you into my life Holy Spirit.

Jesus Christ, come into my heart and life.

Holy Spirit take complete control of my life.

I am a sinner and acknowledge you as my Savior.

In Jesus' Name I pray, Amen.

Acknowledgement

First, I want to give honor and glory to my Lord and Savior Jesus Christ.

Without my wife, this great book ministry would not be possible.

Thanks to my parents, brother and family for their continued support.

Thanks to my Baltimore City Department of Social Services Family.

Thanks to all of my friends that supported me during the journey of completing this book.

A special thanks to Pat Alfin for your insight.

www.ingramcontent.com/pod-product-compliance
Lightning Source LLC
Chambersburg PA
CBHW052114070526
44584CB00017B/2482